D1508571

Everything
You Need to
Know About

Breast Health and Cancer Detection

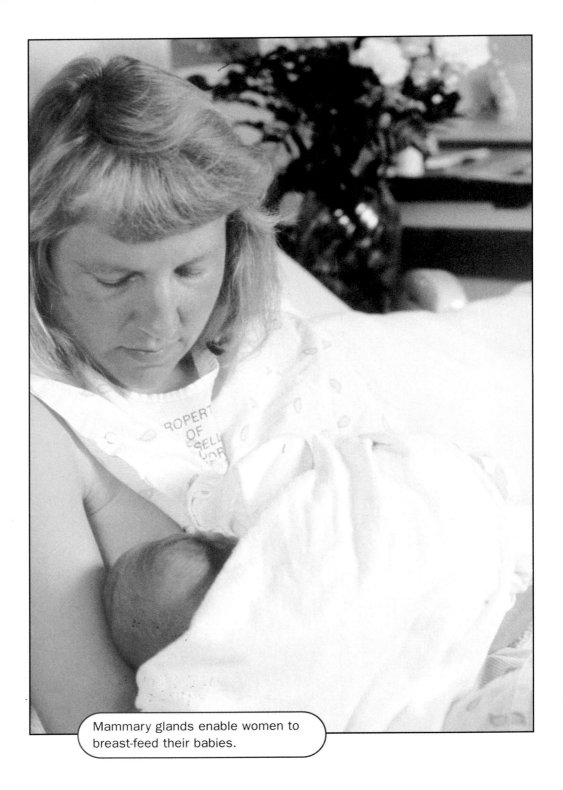

Mammary glands enable women to breast-feed their babies.

Everything You Need to Know About Breast Health and Cancer Detection

Virginia Aronson

The Rosen Publishing Group, Inc.
New York

This book is dedicated to the memory of my mother, Barbara Corrigan Aronson, who died of breast cancer before she was fifty.

Published in 2000 by The Rosen Publishing Group, Inc.
29 East 21st Street, New York, NY 10010

First Edition

Library of Congress Cataloging-in-Publication Data

Aronson, Virginia
  Everything you need to know about breast health and cancer detection / by Virginia Aronson.—1st ed.
     p. cm.—(The need to know library)
Includes bibliographical references and index.
Summary: Explains the basics of breast care and breast health, breast development, and the importance of breast cancer awareness.
    ISBN 0-8239-3224-9 (library binding)
  1. Breast—Care and hygiene—Juvenile literature. 2. Breast—Cancer—Juvenile literature. 3. Breast—Examination—Juvenile literature. [1. Breast—Care and hygiene. 2. Breast—Cancer. 3. Cancer. 4. Diseases.] I. Title. II. Series.
  RG492 .A76 2000
  618. 1'9—dc21
                                                    00-008726

Manufactured in the United States of America.

Contents

Introduction

I'm frightened. My right breast feels lumpy and I'm afraid to ask anyone what this means.

My breasts are small. Is sixteen too young to have plastic surgery?

My mother had breast cancer. Does this mean I'll get it, too?

Breasts are one of the more visible symbols of femininity. When they first begin to develop you may feel a mixture of pride, confusion, and fear. Like getting your first period, the sudden appearance of budding breasts can serve as the first sign of your entry into womanhood. It may also be the beginning of a lifelong struggle with self-acceptance.

Despite the significant advancements brought about by the women's liberation movement, our society has remained old-fashioned when it comes to female sexuality. Female breasts are still regarded as X-rated and, by law, they must be covered in public. Most municipal beaches require swimsuit tops for women. In some areas of the country, mothers can't breast-feed their babies in public places.

Unlike the perfect images portrayed in movies and magazines, real women's breasts come in all sizes and shapes—oftentimes with one larger than the other. In adolescence, being flat-chested is normal and does not mean that you will be small-breasted for life. Some girls have hair around their nipples and some have inverted nipples (the tips do not protrude). Both of these conditions are totally normal.

Teens with well-developed breasts may feel awkward. And girls with family members who have been diagnosed with breast cancer can become anxious about their own health, fearful of their rapidly developing bodies. Once you understand your body, however, you will realize the truth: It is your body and you can make it work for you, while enhancing your self-image and empowering yourself as a woman—a confident, healthy woman.

Although serious breast disease is uncommon in very young women, and breast cancer is extremely rare in teenagers, it is important to learn how to examine

Developing breasts is a sign of a girl's entry into womanhood.

your breasts for what may be an abnormality. If you get to know your breasts now, and continue to be familiar with them as they grow, develop, and change throughout your life, you should be able to spot a problem early—and get help right away.

Nikki Uberti, a popular grunge-chic model, was only twenty-eight years old when she found a lump in one of her breasts. Her grandmother had died at thirty-nine and her mother at forty-one, both from breast cancer. "Like everyone, I wanted to believe that this was not happening to me," Nikki said in a 1999 *Allure* article. "I guess I tried to believe that it was OK."

In Nikki's case, the breast lump was, in fact, not okay. Even though her story is unusual, breast cancer awareness at an early age is very important. A basic understanding of proper breast care for lifelong breast health can save your life, as it did for Nikki.

This book will tell you the facts you need to know about breast care and breast health. Reading the chapters that follow will help you become more familiar and comfortable with your breasts in order to keep them healthy—for life.

Chapter One

Know Your Breasts

*W*hen Kate was almost thirteen, she got her first period. A week or so before she began menstruating, her breasts had felt very tender. They were so sore she could hardly run during gym class. Kate decided to tell her mother what was going on, even though it was embarrassing and awkward for her.

Kate's mom was totally cool about it. She explained that breast tenderness was perfectly normal and that it happened to her, too. She offered to purchase a sports bra for Kate and asked whether she wanted to learn how to do a breast self-examination to familiarize herself with how her breasts feel. That way, Kate's mom reassured her, she could be certain that her *breasts were healthy, even when they felt tender or lumpy.*

Kate's mother demonstrated how to conduct the exam by letting Kate watch her check her own breasts. It looked pretty easy, so Kate tried it, too. Simple! When Kate got home from school the next day, there was a shopping bag on her bed: The sports bra fit great, and the tampons came in handy several days later when Kate's period started.

Although you'll hear many silly nicknames for women's breasts, the mammary glands—or milk-producing organs—are simply another part of the woman's reproductive system. To know your breasts is to care for them—and you are the person who will know them the best.

In contrast to the flawless and perky breasts that we see on magazine models and movie stars, real-life bosoms come in a wide variety of shapes and sizes. Your breasts, like your face, are uniquely you. And, like much of the rest of you, your breasts will change throughout your lifetime.

It is your responsibility to get to know your own body so that you can keep it healthy. This means becoming familiar with the breasts you have, their cyclical changes, and individual development, as you grow and mature.

A sports bra can protect your breasts during gym class.

What Is Normal For You

Do you think the following statements are true or false?

- Both of your breasts should be exactly the same bra cup size.

- The way your breasts are in your late teens is the way they will be forever.

- Hairy nipples are abnormal, due to some kind of hormonal imbalance.

- Nipples should be brown with tips that point straight ahead.

None of these statements is true. Surprised? Believe it or not, most women have one breast that is slightly larger than the other. If the difference in size is one bra cup or more, you can always buy the larger size bra and pad one of the cups to create a more balanced look.

The rate at which breasts grow varies from person to person, sometimes with one breast developing at a faster pace than the other. Many girls' breasts grow in spurts, and these growth spurts can keep on occurring into your late teens, twenties, and even your thirties.

Your breasts may look even or uneven in size until age sixteen or later. They may be noticeably budding as early as eight or nine. They may be round, or pear or teardrop-shaped. No two breasts are shaped the same way. Your genes will determine most of these factors.

However, your body weight has a big influence on your bustline as well. If you gain extra body fat, your breasts will increase in size (about one-third of breast tissue is fat tissue). If you lose weight, your breasts will probably become smaller, as well.

As your hormones change during your lifetime, your breasts may change, too. With pregnancy and aging, your breasts will probably get larger, fuller, and eventually, more saggy. So whatever your breasts look like today, they are likely to look different next year and in the years to follow.

Nipples, like breasts, vary from person to person. Some women may have a bit of hair on the areola, which is the darker area surrounding the nipple. This is perfectly normal and natural. The areola looks different in different women, varying widely in color and size. Fair-haired women typically have pinkish areolas, while those of dark-haired women and African Americans look brown or black. Nipples usually point toward the armpits, as this creates the easiest access for a suckling baby cradled in its mother's arms.

A Breast Self-Exam Is Easy

Examining your breasts on a regular basis need not be a dull chore or a frightening task you do specifically to hunt for cancerous lumps. A breast self-exam, or BSE, can teach you about your body and its ongoing changes as you grow. Practicing a BSE can help you become more comfortable with yourself. And comfort with your body is a large factor in high self-esteem.

As an adult, you may want to conduct a BSE every month, which is what most health experts recommend. As a teenager, however, this is probably not necessary. But it will be easier to remember to do if you practice your BSE on a regular basis, like a few days after your menstrual period ends.

The U.S. Department of Health and Human Services recommends the following method for a BSE:

1. Stand before a mirror. Inspect both breasts for anything unusual, such as any discharge from the nipples, puckering, dimpling, or scaling of the skin.

   (The next two steps are designed to emphasize any change in the shape or contour of your breasts. As you do these exercises you should be able to feel your chest muscles tighten.)

2. Watching closely in the mirror, clasp hands behind your head and press hands forward.

3. Next, press hands firmly on hips and bow

Breast Self-Examination

In the shower, keep one hand over-head and examine each breast with the opposite hand.

Lying in bed, place a pillow under one shoulder to elevate and flatten breast. Examine each breast with opposite hand, first with arm under head and again with arm at side.

In front of a mirror, stand with hands resting on hips. Examine breasts for swelling, dimpling, bulges, and changes in skin.

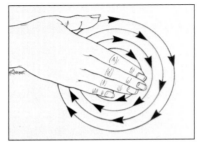

Make rotary motions—with flat pads, not tips of fingers—in concentric circle inward toward nipple. Feel for knobs, lumps, or indentations. Be sure to include the armpit area.

In front of mirror, with arms extended overhead, examine breasts for changes. This position high-lights bulges and indentations that may indicate a lump.

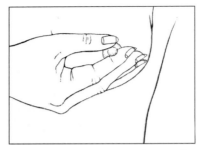

Squeeze nipples gently to inspect for any discharge. Report any suspicious findings to your doctor.

slightly toward the mirror as you pull your shoulders and elbows forward.

(Some women do the next part of the exam in the shower. Fingers glide over soapy skin, making it easy to concentrate on the texture underneath.)

4. Raise your left arm. Use three or four fingers of your right hand to explore your left breast firmly, carefully, and thoroughly. Beginning at the outer edge of the breast, press the flat part of your fingers in small circles, moving the circles slowly around the breast. Gradually work toward the nipple. Be sure to cover the entire breast. Pay special attention to the area between the breast and the armpit, including the armpit itself. Feel for any unusual lump or mass under the skin.

5. Gently squeeze the nipple and look for discharge. Repeat the exam on your right breast.

Steps 4 and 5 should be repeated lying down. Lie flat on your back, left arm over your head and a pillow or folded towel under your left shoulder. This position flattens the breast and makes it easier to examine. Use the same circular motion described earlier. Repeat on your right breast.

If you are not sure how to examine your breasts yourself or are not comfortable with it, you can always rely on a doctor to do the BSE for you. Once you've begun to develop, each time you visit a gynecologist or your family physician for a regular checkup, he or she will examine your breasts for any abnormalities. It is unlikely that you or your doctor will find anything out of the ordinary, but the next chapter will tell you what you need to know about the most common—but harmless—breast problems.

Chapter Two

No-Problem Breast Problems

*I*n the shower one morning, Jessica soaped her breasts more thoroughly than usual, and suddenly she felt a big lump in her right breast! She turned off the water and rushed out to the living room in a panic.

Jessica's grandmother was able to calm her enough so that she could return to the shower, rinse off, and dress. Jessica was sure that she had cancer. Only fourteen and already her life was over! Jessica insisted on making an appointment to see the family doctor right away!

When Dr. Alyson informed her that there was nothing abnormal about her breast, Jessica didn't believe it. Surely the lump was unhealthy, cancerous, dangerous? But after Dr. Alyson helped Jessica examine both of her breasts *properly, she realized that the "tumor" was actually just part of her normal body: a ridge of fat lying underneath each of her perfectly healthy breasts.*

If she hadn't been so relieved, Jessica would have felt like a complete idiot. She promised Dr. Alyson that she would do regular self-exams so that she could avoid future panic attacks.

At least once in your lifetime, you will probably notice something about your breasts that doesn't seem right. You may panic or immediately begin to deny the possibility of a problem with your health. Either way, you may feel uncomfortable, frightened, and confused. However, it may be reassuring to know that most women experience such breast scares and, for most of us, it turns out that there is nothing to worry about. But just to make certain there is no problem, it's always a good idea to see a doctor.

Your "Normal" Breasts

According to biologists, a "normal" female breast is one that can produce breast milk. All mammals have mammary glands, which enables females to breast-feed their babies. Human females have two mammary glands. Large or small, even or uneven, as long as a set of breasts produces milk for a newborn baby, they are regarded as medically normal.

Mammary glands are the distinguishing trait of all mammals.

Breast Variations

There are many variations within the definition of normal. One common variation is the extra nipple—an evolutionary leftover from the days when humans were more like other mammals who often have multiple pairs of nipples. A few women actually have extra breast tissue, without a nipple, typically located under the armpit. Unless these "extras" cause physical discomfort or psychological stress, there is no need to have them surgically removed.

Another normal variation is the diverse sizes of breasts, which is often hereditary. "Large" is a subjective term, however, because many women are comfortable with a size 36C while others, especially petite girls,

During the 1920s, it was fashionable for women to be as flat-chested as men.

might feel burdened and/or inhibited. The opposite variation is equally as subjective because being "flat-chested" or small-breasted can depend on both the opinion of the observer and the cultural values of the era. During the 1920s, for example, the fashion of the times dictated that it was attractive to be as flat-chested as a male, prompting women to bind their chests. These days, surgically enhanced breasts are "in," which has led to a boom in the business of cosmetic surgery. The potential dangers of this procedure will be discussed in chapter 4.

Some women have permanently inverted nipples, which are nipples that have grown inward instead of outward. A simple surgical procedure can reverse this condition, but the results of surgery can prove to be merely temporary, with the nipples spontaneously returning to their inverted position.

Despite the many variations, it is important to accept your perfectly normal breasts the way they are; after all, they are a part of you.

Breast Behavior

As you near or enter your teens, you will come up against the typically challenging life-cycle stage known as puberty. Hair begins to appear in your armpits and pubic area, your period starts, and your breasts begin to grow. Chemical messengers in the body, called hormones, trigger these steps toward sexual maturity.

WHEN?	WHAT?	WHY?
During or just after your period (Days 1–7):	Your breasts are full, tender, and sore but begin to return to normal by Day 3 or 4.	The hormones that started your period are shutting down.
Post-period (Days 8–14):	Your breasts are normal, no swelling or soreness.	The hormones are low.
Mid-cycle (Days 15–20):	Your breasts begin to get fuller and more sensitive.	The hormones are revving up again.
Just before your period (Days 21–28):	Your breasts get more swollen, sore, possibly lumpy.	Hormones are high, starting up your period once again.

For females, the hormones estrogen and progesterone are most influential. And as the levels of these hormones in the body naturally increase and begin to fluctuate, obvious physical and emotional changes occur. In addition to feeling alternately cranky and on top of the world, you'll experience changes in your breast size and texture.

By learning to recognize the regularity of these physical and psychological changes, you'll begin to understand your body's cycles. Once you see the pattern—and understand that it is normal and healthy— you may feel more comfortable with your ever-changing body and psyche. You can use the chart below to tune in to the typical pattern for monthly breast changes as you begin to recognize your own special cycle.

Lumps and Bumps

You'll be relieved to know that tender, lumpy breasts are normal at certain times of the month. But what if your breasts feel *extremely* lumpy? Or what if, when you squeeze your nipples, some fluid oozes out? Or suddenly there's a big bump on one breast that feels either rock-hard or squishy? Are these abnormalities the symptoms of breast cancer?

The Facts

As a teenager, it is unlikely that any lumps or bumps will turn out to be cancerous. In fact, only one out of every 20,000 women under the age of twenty-five will be diagnosed with breast cancer. If you find something unusual in your breast, don't hesitate to make an appointment with your doctor for reassurance.

Normal lumpiness is due to the different types of tissue that make up your breasts: The milk-producing glands, structural tissue, and fat each have a different texture. Normal lumpiness feels like bunches of thickened tissue, not like a separate and distinct bump, which is usually something other than breast tissue.

If your doctor informs you that your lumpy breasts are due to "fibrocystic disease" or "cystic mastitis," don't get nervous. These terms are actually old-fashioned labels that merely indicate your breast lumps are normal and noncancerous. Most "treatments" for the lumpiness are ineffective, but some women do achieve relief by reducing or eliminating their intake of caffeine. If your lumps bother you, try cutting back on or cutting out all caffeinated products, such as coffee, tea, colas, and chocolate. If your lumps don't bother you, there is no need to treat them.

Some women experience breast pain, with or without lumps. This, too, is normal but it can be annoying. Although no treatment has proven effective, reducing the extra fat in your diet may make a difference. This means cutting down on red meats, fried foods, fast foods, and rich desserts. More on diet and breast health is included in chapter 5.

Less Common Conditions

Breast infections and nipple discharge are less common problems. These conditions need to be checked by your doctor. But rest assured, breast infections and discharges do *not* cause cancer.

If you ever discover a smooth, round, hard lump in one of your breasts, don't panic. Chances are the lump is a "fibroadenoma," or noncancerous tumor. Teenagers are prone to developing harmless lumps, which can be the size of a pea or a marble. Your doctor can usually tell just by feeling the growth if it is a fibroadenoma, which will move around freely in the breast tissue. He or she may recommend that your fibroadenoma be surgically removed, primarily so you won't keep worrying about it.

Cysts are more common in women who are in their thirties, forties, and early fifties. These squishy or hard fluid-filled sacs typically appear overnight, which can be a pretty scary discovery. A doctor will use a needle to drain out the fluid, immediately collapsing the cyst. Most cysts are a harmless nuisance and, like fibroadenomas, do not increase the risk for cancer. Nonetheless, you should still have them checked out by a doctor.

Wake-Up Call

MacKenzie woke up early and jumped out of bed, stripping off her pajama top as she headed for the shower. Suddenly she froze. What was that thing on her left breast? MacKenzie stood before the bathroom mirror and stared. There it was, a BB-size bump, right near her nipple.

27

After showering and dressing for school, MacKenzie telephoned her mother's office. They agreed that the lump was probably a harmless cyst, but MacKenzie's mother advised her to get an appointment at the free clinic to check it out.

The clinic gynecologist informed MacKenzie that the lump was a fibroadenoma and asked whether she wanted to have it removed—a simple surgical procedure that could be performed by a surgeon on an outpatient basis. MacKenzie said that she would discuss the matter with her mother. She knew that the lump wasn't breast cancer and would not become cancerous, so she didn't feel rushed to make a decision.

After discussing the issue with her mom and with her best friend, whose stepsister's mother had been diagnosed with breast cancer in her late thirties, MacKenzie scheduled an appointment with the surgeon recommended by the free clinic. If she left the lump on her breast, it would always be there. And since MacKenzie didn't want to waste any more time worrying about it, she opted for the surgery.

Chapter Three

Breast Cancer— Diagnosis and Prevention

Although it is true that breast cancer is a terrible disease and a leading killer of women in the United States, what is even more dangerous is the widespread fear of getting it. Even though you will hopefully never have to face a diagnosis of breast cancer, you should arm yourself with the important and useful facts. By being informed, you can be sure to avoid or overcome unnecessary anxiety regarding this widely misunderstood disease.

Myths versus Facts

There are indeed some scary statistics about breast cancer, but most of the information surrounding the disease is more myth than fact. Take a look at each of the common breast cancer myths that follow, then compare them with the facts. Getting the disease in proper perspective can enable you to turn fear into wisdom, saving you years of needless worry, confusion, and even panic.

Myth: Breast cancer is the number-one killer of women in the United States.

Heart disease kills ten times as many women as breast cancer does every year. More women die from lung cancer (primarily due to cigarette smoking) than breast cancer. Even though the statistics do look bad—more than 175,000 American women are diagnosed with breast cancer each year, and around 46,000 a year will die from it—the full facts are less frightening. With more than 138 million women and girls living in the United States, the percent of the total to be diagnosed with breast cancer is actually around .13 percent, or just over one-tenth of 1 percent.

Myth: Breast cancer is primarily a young woman's disease.

The only factors proven to increase your risk for developing breast cancer are being a woman (men do get the disease, but very rarely) and aging. When you are under the age of twenty-five, your chances of getting the disease are less than one in 20,000. But as you grow older, your risk slowly increases—as it does for many other diseases, such as heart disease and diabetes. When you hear that one in eight women will get breast cancer, this really means one in eight women over the age of eighty-five. Furthermore, more than three out of four patients diagnosed with the disease are age fifty or older. The chart below shows the details of your lifetime risk for breast cancer.

Your Real Risk*

By age, your risk for breast cancer is:

AGE	RISK	AGE	RISK
25	1 in 19,608	70	1 in 14
35	1 in 622	75	1 in 11
45	1 in 93	80	1 in 10
55	1 in 33	85	1 in 9
65	1 in 17	lifetime	1 in 8

*Adapted from the National Cancer Institute Surveillance Program

Myth: More young women are dying from breast cancer than ever before.

During the 1990s, the number of breast cancer deaths in women under forty declined, as did the death statistics for women with breast cancer in all age groups.

Myth: If your mother or grandmother had breast cancer, you will probably get it, too.

Around 80 percent of the women who are diagnosed with breast cancer do not have a mother, sister, or daughter with the disease. It is true that your risk increases if you have a close blood relative with breast cancer, but the vast majority of breast cancers are not

Although a healthy lifestyle cannot guarantee a life without breast cancer, it can reduce the risk.

hereditary. The kind of breast cancer that is due to a genetic flaw (and therefore may—or may not—be inherited) is quite rare, accounting for only 5 to 10 percent of all breast cancer cases.

Myth: People who regularly eat right and exercise do not get cancer.

Unfortunately, this is not always true. Although scientific studies indicate that certain lifestyle factors may reduce the chances for developing some cancers, including breast cancer, there are people who eat healthfully and participate in vigorous physical activity who do contract cancer.

Living Healthy

There is no surefire way to prevent breast cancer. However, medical evidence supports a probable link between your behavior and your risk for certain cancers, such as breast cancer. This means you might want to make the lifestyle changes that scientists believe could make a difference in the long run. After all, living a healthy life can only help.

More on this and other steps toward cancer prevention and lifelong breast health are included in chapter 5.

Mammograms

You may have heard of or read about the medical screening procedure called the mammogram. This is a photograph of your breasts made by special X rays that detect very small breast lumps which cannot be felt by hand. As

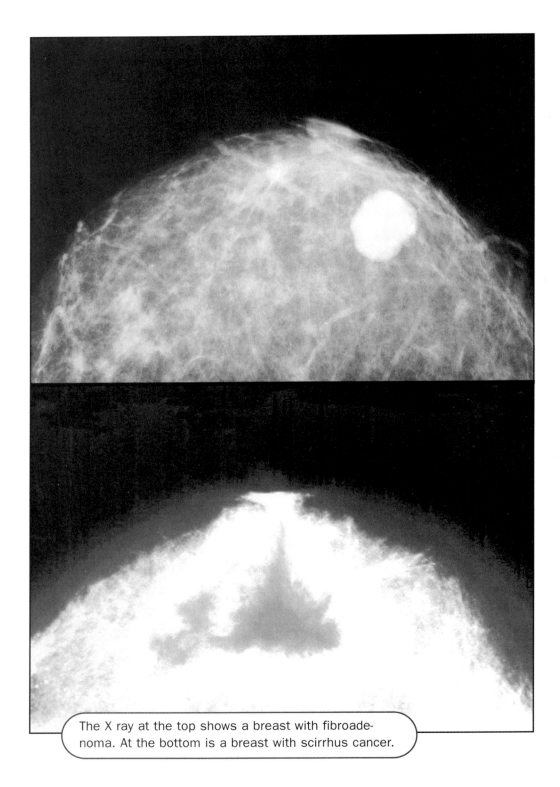

The X ray at the top shows a breast with fibroadenoma. At the bottom is a breast with scirrhus cancer.

a teenager, a mammogram is *not* recommended. Young women's breast tissue is so dense that these X rays are unable to reveal anything. You will probably not need a mammogram until you are thirty-five years old. If you have a family history of breast cancer, however, your doctor may urge you to get a mammogram earlier.

By the time *you* are in your thirties or forties, however, there will probably be newer, more accurate screening tests and other proven preventive measures that will be recommended for breast health. And with the successful advances that are expected for cancer research, treatment, and prevention over the next two decades, fewer women will have reason to fear the disease. With all that you know now, you can choose to be cautious, careful, and free of anxiety when it comes to the health of your breasts.

Nikki's Case

Nikki Uberti, the young model who developed breast cancer, states in the *Allure* article that she discovered the first lump early. "I wasn't even giving myself an exam. Because I am so skinny, you could see it protruding when I lay down. It felt like a little pea." She went to see her doctor at once. Because Nikki was so young, her gynecologist did not do a mammogram. Unfortunately, Nikki and her doctor failed to discuss her family history of breast cancer. Instead, she was reassured that the lump was benign, but Nikki intuitively felt that something was wrong.

When two more lumps appeared in the same breast, Nikki sought out a second opinion. She was given a biopsy—a procedure in which tissue was surgically removed—to test for cancerous growth. One week before her thirtieth birthday, Nikki was told that she had breast cancer.

At first, she cried. But then, she realized she had to focus on her recovery and health. Of her change in attitude, she says, "you find out and you fight. And be positive. And you can win. Plenty of women win. I just plan on being one of them."

Nikki had to have a mastectomy, which is the surgical removal of a breast. Then she changed her life. She cut out all red meat, stopped drinking alcohol, and blew off a seventeen-year cigarette habit. "I was wild," she has admitted, "like a normal twentysomething-year-old. But I stopped it all, overnight."

These days, Nikki Uberti works at regaining her health. She prays. And she makes plans for the future: "I have dreams, and I want to get back to them as soon as I can." Nikki is currently working on her acting skills in the hopes of becoming an actress as well as a model.

Nikki's story is unusual because young women rarely develop breast cancer. Yet her case is not so unusual in that she has a good prognosis: Most women who are diagnosed with breast cancer have a very good chance of survival.

Celebrities Who Beat Breast Cancer:

- Carly Simon, singer
- Olivia Newton-John, actress and singer
- Jill Eikenberry, actress (*LA Law*)
- Kate Jackson, actress (*Charlie's Angels*)
- Julia Child, TV chef
- Linda Ellerbee, TV anchor
- Diahann Carroll, actress
- Shirley Temple Black, actress and politician
- Gloria Steinem, feminist
- Betty Ford, former first lady (wife of Gerald Ford)
- Happy Rockefeller, wife of former vice president Nelson Rockefeller
- Nancy Reagan, former first lady (wife of Ronald Reagan)
- Sandra Day O'Connor, U.S. Supreme Court Justice
- Peggy Fleming, Olympic figure skater

Chapter Four

Breast Implants—Boost or Bust?

In October 1999, pop singer Britney Spears felt compelled to make a public announcement about the size of her breasts. In order to combat the rumors that surgical implants were behind her noticeably bigger bustline, the seventeen-year-old celebrity revealed the truth. It was a growth spurt—so common in girls her age— along with a twenty-five-pound weight gain. "In some interviews I would just start crying," the young superstar said in a recent newspaper article about the gossip focusing on her breasts. "I'd be like, 'Why are you being so rude to me?'"

Conforming to the standards of beauty valued in one's culture can be difficult and uncomfortable, even painful or unhealthy. And since the cultural ideals for feminine beauty typically are different from what is

Pop singer Britney Spears denies that she had surgical breast implants.

Actress Pamela Anderson Lee had her breast implants removed.

normal and common, many women, in seeking to attain these standards, often undermine their own sense of self-worth.

Actress Pamela Anderson Lee decided in the spring of 1999 that she no longer wished to have the attention-grabbing breasts that were her trademark. So the former *Baywatch* beauty underwent surgery to remove her breast implants, announcing afterward in a *People* magazine article, "It's something I've been wanting to do for a long time." Fellow actress Sally Kirkland, who had her own implants removed a few years earlier when they began leaking, commended the buxom star in the same article for "giving the message to young women that it's time to accept themselves."

Double Trouble

Like Lee, many women who opt for surgical enhancement instead of self-acceptance end up regretting their choice. Yet the use of breast implants is booming, increasing in popularity despite a great deal of negative press about complications.

According to the American Society of Plastic and Reconstructive Surgeons, the number of breast-implant operations more than doubled between 1992 and 1996, with an estimated 90,000 women receiving surgically enlarged breasts in 1996 alone. Complications from the surgery—in which synthetic baggies

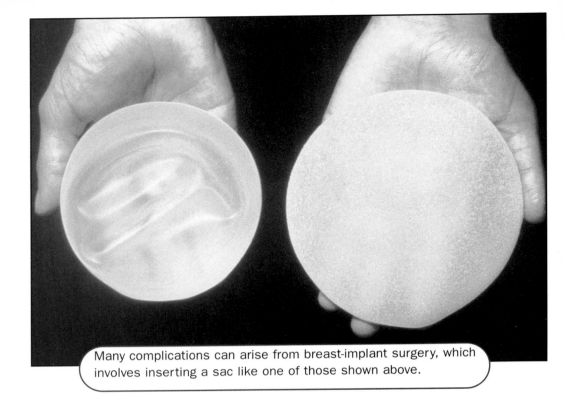

Many complications can arise from breast-implant surgery, which involves inserting a sac like one of those shown above.

made from silicone and filled with saline, or salt water, are inserted under or over the chest muscles—include infection, bleeding, deflation, and hardening of the scar tissue. Sometimes the implants leak, which some health experts and many women believe to be dangerous to health. Mammograms can prove difficult to read and interpret after one has had breast implants, which can result in the failure to detect cancer.

In 1992 the United States government banned the use of silicone gel filler in breast implants (although the baggies are still made from it) because of the huge number of complaints that it caused a variety of health problems. Actress Mary McDonough, who played Erin, John-Boy Walton's sister on the popular TV series *The Waltons,* believes that her long-term, serious health problems are due to the silicone breast implants she got in 1984. "After the show ended [in 1981, when she was twenty-one], I didn't have very good self-esteem," the thirty-six-year-old actress told *People* magazine in 1997. "I was always trying to be thin for my work. I had friends who were getting implants, and it seemed like a fun thing to do."

The strange illnesses that appeared after her surgery, however, were anything but fun: Flulike fevers, joint stiffness, rashes, and shooting muscle pains, plus an unshakable fatigue, shortened the talented actress's career. In 1994, when McDonough had her implants removed, the surgeon found that the shells had disintegrated, allowing the silicone to circulate throughout her body.

So far, scientific studies have failed to prove the existence of a link between silicone in the body and the various illnesses some women experience after receiving breast implants. But the risks associated with this type of surgery are obvious. And the benefits are questionable. As Mary McDonough explains in that same article, "There was a hole inside me. I thought if I were thin, if I had big breasts, that would fill the hole. But it wasn't until I got rid of the big breasts that I realized what was missing—my voice. Communication. And loving myself."

Misleading Images

The large, prominent breasts found on the superthin bodies of models, actresses, and centerfolds are not always natural. And they feel as artificial as they are—like waterbeds, unnaturally cool and bound up tight in plastic, sometimes hard to the touch.

Certainly, the business of plastic surgery profits from our current cultural obsession with surgically enhanced breasts. True, some women do feel better about themselves after surgical enhancement, be it breast enlargement or a nose job, liposuction (body fat removal), or a face-lift. But most women still opt for a more natural, less risky approach to self-acceptance and self-esteem.

In a recent magazine article, one hundred readers were polled to find out what girls thought of their own breasts. They discovered that 68 percent thought they would never get breast enlargement surgery—even if the operation was free—although almost half of those surveyed would prefer to have bigger boobs. More than 40 percent condemned breast implants as an "unsafe and totally stupid thing to do to yourself."

Chapter Five

The Best Breasts Are Healthy Breasts

When Victoria was seventeen, her thirty-nine-year-old mother died from breast cancer. A few months later, Victoria began reading a book about nutrition and health that a friend had recommended. She became convinced that if she adopted a super-healthy lifestyle, she would be able to avoid her mother's tragic fate.

Victoria transformed her life: She became a strict vegetarian, avoided eating fried foods and junk foods, and began taking various vitamins and herbs. She jogged every day. She stayed away from alcohol of all kinds, recreational drugs, and cigarettes. She was pleased with her lean, muscular body and firm bustline. But she was still afraid that one day she, too, would find a lump in her breast.

Then the unthinkable happened. During a regular breast self-exam, Victoria discovered a hard lump the size of a pebble. She felt a curious mixture of fear and relief. At least she would no longer be waiting for her fate. She was thirty-two, and ready to face her destiny.

When the doctor informed Victoria that the lump was a fibroadenoma, she began to weep. Perhaps she was not destined to repeat her mother's tragedy after all, but to live out her own unique journey.

At her fortieth birthday party, Victoria had two glasses of champagne, one in honor of her mother and the other to celebrate her health. On her fiftieth birthday, she climbed Mount Washington with her two daughters. And on her sixtieth birthday, Victoria participated in a local 10-kilometer race to benefit a national breast cancer research fund. She came in first in her age group.

Victoria's story is not uncommon. Many women who have lost their mothers or close relatives to breast cancer are fearful that they, too, will contract the disease. Rosie O'Donnell has been admirably candid in discussing her mother, who died of breast cancer when the popular comedienne was a child. O'Donnell has used her television talk show, the Emmy-winning *Rosie O'Donnell Show*, as a platform to educate viewers about breast health. As she explains in her irreverently honest and straight-to-the-funny-bone style, "It seems plain that the more we know, the better equipped we will be to live life together with our boobs instead of in fear of them."

Facts Instead of Fear

So what do you need to know in order to keep your breasts fit and your mind at ease? You've already read the basic facts about breasts and breast health in the preceding chapters. You now know how to do a breast self-exam and how important it is to conduct a BSE on a regular basis. Right now, once in a while is fine. By the time you are twenty, however, you should be doing a monthly BSE.

You also know that most of the breast lumps and bumps you'll find are normal and are nothing to worry about. But if you do discover a distinct lump or anything else that seems abnormal to you, you are now aware that it is always a good idea to be examined by your gynecologist or family doctor.

You probably realize the risks involved in breast enlargement surgery. And you should understand the psychological value that lies in accepting your body as it is—with the recognition that your breasts will change over time. Perhaps you have even grown a bit fonder of your breasts as you have familiarized yourself with your own unique physique.

A well-balanced diet including lots of fruits and vegetables is an important factor in a healthy lifestyle.

Healthy Choices

Since you are aware that the chances of being diagnosed with breast cancer at your age are pretty slim, you may feel less fearful of the disease. However, this does not mean that you should ignore the need to make healthy life choices now. Scientific studies indicate that successful prevention of breast cancer may begin very early in life. The choices you make today affect the health of your breasts in the future. And since the lifestyle factors that appear to best protect your breasts from disease are also good for your health in general, it makes sense to opt for the healthy choices now. By the time you are old enough to be at some risk for breast cancer, healthful living will be a normal, natural part of your life.

Medical experts recommend the following measures to best protect your breasts while maximizing your overall health:

- *Eat a well-balanced diet.* Include lots of fruits and vegetables, and keep your intake of fried foods, red meats, and junk food to a minimum.

- *Exercise.* Find physical activities you enjoy doing, then do them on a regular basis. Make exercise a fun part of your routine.

- *Avoid becoming overweight.* No need to diet, just adopt the two suggestions above and you should naturally stay in shape.

- *Avoid alcoholic beverages.* Some studies indicate there may be a link between drinking alcohol and an increased risk for breast cancer. Many studies have linked alcohol to a host of other diseases and problems.

- *Do not smoke cigarettes or other tobacco products.* Like alcohol, smoking cigarettes or other tobacco products has been linked to breast cancer.

Smoking cigarettes has been linked to breast cancer and many other health problems.

Although medical research has failed to find an association between the intake of caffeine and breast health problems, there are lots of women who report that reducing their consumption of caffeinated products such as coffee, tea, colas, and chocolate helps reduce tenderness and lumpiness in the breasts. If you suffer from tender and/or lumpy breasts, you might try staying away from caffeinated products and see if that helps.

Body Piercing

Piercing has recently become a popular form of body adornment. However, it is risky, because whenever you pierce the skin, you open your body up to infection and permanent damage. This is especially important to be aware of because there are few laws and regulations governing the practice of body piercing (and tattooing). Health and safety precautions can vary dramatically from place to place. If you do ever decide to have any area of your body pierced, be certain that the place where you choose to get your work done follows very strict sanitary practices.

If you are considering having your nipples pierced, you should also consider the risks. As mentioned, with any body piercing there is always risk of infection as well as pain, bleeding, and permanent scarring. A risk specific to nipple-piercing is a partial or total loss of sensitivity in the nipple which, once inflicted, is irreversible.

The decision to pierce your body is always up to you, but it is important to know the risks so that you can make informed choices. And always, the most important factors to keep in mind are your health and feelings of self-acceptance.

Glossary

areola Area around the nipple that appears darker than the rest of the breast.

benign Not cancerous.

biopsy Removal of tissue, surgically or with a needle, for testing purposes.

breast implants Sacs filled with salt water inside rubber-like shells that are surgically inserted behind breast tissue to enlarge the breast.

caffeine Chemical substance found in coffee, teas, some soft drinks, and chocolate; works as a stimulant in the body, increasing alertness.

cancer Abnormal cell growth resulting in a variety of diseases.

cyst Fluid-filled sac.

estrogen Female sex hormone produced in varying amounts throughout the reproductive cycle.

fibroadenoma   Benign tumor of the breast common in young women.

fibrocystic disease   Outdated term used for lumpy breasts; merely indicates lumps are benign.

genes   Cell material or units responsible for heredity as well as the day-to-day functions and reproduction of all cells in the body.

genetic   Related to the genes and/or to inherited characteristics.

gynecologist   Physician who specializes in the reproductive health of women.

hormones   Chemicals, produced by glands in the body, that travel through the bloodstream and influence various body tissues and functions.

liposuction   Surgical removal of excess body fat by means of suction.

mammary glands   Glands in the breasts that, in females, produce and secrete milk.

mammogram   X-ray photograph used to detect breast cancer.

mastectomy   Surgery to remove the breast(s) and some surrounding tissues.

progesterone   Female hormone involved in the menstrual cycle.

prognosis   The predicted outcome of a disease or disorder.

puberty   The stage during physical and sexual maturation when the body becomes capable of reproduction.

silicone   Synthetic material used in breast implants.

synthetic   Artificial substance not found in nature.

Where to
Go for Help

In the United States

American College of Obstetricians
    and Gynecologists
409 12th Street, SW
Washington, DC 20090-6920
(202) 638-5577
Web site: http://www.acog.org

Helping Children Cope Program
Cancer Care, Inc.
275 7th Avenue
New York, NY 10001
(800) 813-HOPE
Web site: http://www.cancercare.org

Just for Teens
Y-Me National Breast Cancer Organization
212 West Van Buren
Chicago, IL 60607-3907
(800) 221-2141
Web site: http://www.y-me.org

Kids Count Too
American Cancer Society
15999 Clifton Road, NE
Atlanta, GA 30329
(800) ACS-2345
Web site: http://www.cancer.org

Kids Konnected (support for children of
        mothers with breast cancer)
27071 Cabot Road, Suite 102
Laguna Hills, CA 92653
(800) 899-2866
Web site: http://www.kidskonnected.org

The Susan G. Komen Breast Cancer Foundation
5005 LBJ Freeway, Suite 370
Dallas, TX 75244
(800) 462-9273
Web site: http://www.breastcancerinfo.com

National Cancer Institute
Building 31, Room 10A 03
31 Center Drive, MSC 2580
Bethesda, MD 20892
(800) 4-CANCER
Web site: http://www.nci.nih.gov/

National Center for Complementary
        and Alternative Medicine
National Institutes of Health
P.O. Box 8218
Silver Spring, MD 20907-8218
(888) 644-6226
Web site: http://www.altmed.od.nih.gov/

National Women's Health Information Center
A Project of the Office on Women's Health
U.S. Department of Health & Human Services
200 Independence Avenue, SW, Room 730B
Washington, DC 20201
(800) 994-WOMAN
Web site: http://www.4woman.gov

National Women's Health Network
514 10th Street NW, Suite 400
Washington, DC 20004
(202) 347-1140
Web site: http://womenshealthnetwork.org

Office of Women's Health Initiatives
624 Ninth Street, NW, 3rd Floor
Washington, DC 20001
(800) 953-7587

Women's Health Information Center
P.O. Box 192
West Somerville, MA 02144

In Canada

Canadian Breast Cancer Foundation
790 Bay Street, Suite 1000
Toronto, ON M5G 1N8
(800) 387-9816
Web site: http://www.cbcf.org

Canadian Breast Cancer Research Initiative
10 Alcorn Avenue, Suite 200
Toronto, ON M4V 3B1
Web site: http://www.breast.cancer.ca

C.E.R.B.E.
5270 Mills Street
Rock Forest, Quebec J1N 3B6
(819) 564-7883
Web site: http://www.cerbe.com/cerbe

For Further Reading

Boston Women's Health Collective. *Our Bodies, Ourselves for the New Century: A Book by and for Women*. New York: Simon and Schuster, 1992.

Brack, Pat and Ben Brack. *Moms Don't Get Sick*. Pierre, SD: Melius Publishing, 1990.

Brown, Laurie Krasny. *What's the Big Secret: Talking about Sex with Girls and Boys*. Boston: Little, Brown, 1997.

Clifford, Christine. *Our Family Has Cancer Too!* Duluth, MN: Pfeifer-Hamilton Publishers, 1997.

Davidson, James. *In Touch with Your Breasts: The Answers to Women's Questions about Breast Care*. Waco, TX: WRS Group, 2000.

Diamond, Shifra. *Everything You Need to Know About Going to the Gynecologist.* New York: The Rosen Publishing Group, 1999.

Eisenpreis, Bettijane. *Coping: A Young Woman's Guide to Breast Cancer Prevention.* New York: The Rosen Publishing Group, 1997.

Love, Susan, and Karen Lindsey. *Dr. Susan Love's Breast Book.* Reading, MA: Addison-Wesley, 1990.

O'Donnell, Rosie, and Deborah Axelrod. *Bosom Buddies: Lessons and Laughter on Breast Health and Cancer.* New York: Warner Books, 1999.

Smith, William. *A Portrait of Breast Cancer: Expressions in Words and Art.* Atlanta, GA: The American Cancer Society, 1996.

Stoppard, Miriam. *Breast Health.* New York: DK Publishing, 1998.

Vogel, Carole G. *Will I Get Breast Cancer: Questions and Answers for Teenage Girls.* New York: Julian Messner, 1995.

Yagyu, Genichiro. *The Story of Breasts.* Brooklyn, NY: Kane/Miller Book Publishers, 1999.

Index

Index

G
genes, 13, 33
growth spurts, 13, 38
gynecologist, 18, 47

H
hormones, 14, 23–24

K
Kirkland, Sally, 41

L
Lee, Pamela Anderson, 40–41
lifestyle, healthy, 32, 33, 36, 45–46, 48
   recommendations for, 49
lumps in breasts, 8, 11, 16, 17,
    19–20, 25, 33, 35–36
   noncancerous, 25, 26, 27–28, 47
lumpy breasts, 24, 25–26, 51

M
mammogram, 33–35, 42
mastectomy, 36
McDonough, Mary, 42–43
medical advances in future, 35
menstrual period, 6, 10, 15, 23, 24

N
nipple, extra, 21

nipples, 7, 13, 14, 15, 16, 17, 25,
   51–52
nipples, inverted, 7, 23

O
O'Donnell, Rosie, 46–47

P
physician, family, 18, 19, 25, 26,
   35, 47
puberty, 23

R
recovery and survival, 36, 37

S
self-acceptance, 6, 41, 43, 44, 47
silicone gel, 42, 43
Spears, Britney, 38, 39

T
tattooing, 51

U
Uberti, Nikki, 8, 35–36

W
weight, body, 14, 38, 49

About the Author

Virginia Aronson is the author of more than two dozen books, many on medical and health topics including *Everything You Need to Know About Hepatitis* (The Rosen Publishing Group, 2000). She lives in South Florida with her writer husband and their young son.

Acknowledgments

The author wishes to thank the American Cancer Society, the Susan G. Komen Breast Cancer Foundation, and the National Women's Health Information Center for providing free information to all women on breast health; and Rosie O'Donnell for bringing humor to a painfully serious subject.

Photo Credits

Cover and p. 2, 42 © L. Steinmark/Custom Medical Stock Photo; pp. 8, 12 by Maura Boruchow; p. 21 © Super Stock; p. 22 © H. Armstrong Roberts, Inc. Stock Photography; p. 32 © Steve Skjold Photographs; p. 34 top: © Bates, M.D./Custom Medical Stock Photo, bottom: © J. Croyl/Custom Medical Stock Photo; pp. 39, 40 © Everette Collection, Inc.; p. 48 © Harold Sund/Image Bank; p. 50 © Pictor.